Beauty of the Slow Drip

a journey of loss, grief, and healing

Angel K Will

Beauty of the Slow Drip:
a journey of loss, grief, and healing

Copyright ©2023 by Angel K Will
All rights reserved.

ISBN: 978-0-9852269-5-4
　1. Spirituality　2. Poetry

520 East Publishing Co.

Design Elements:
　Claudio Divizia/Shutterstock.com
　Melissa King/Shutterstock.com
　Essl/Shutterstock.com

No part of this publication may be reproduced, stored in a retrieval system, or transmitted in any form or by any means—electronic, mechanical, photocopy, recording, or any other—except for the brief quotations in printed reviews, without the prior permission of the copyright holder. *Exception: poems within this publication may be used for memorial services honoring a loved one.*

Requests for other usage may be directed to Angel K Will at angelkwill.com

Dedication

This book is written as a memorial
for those who have gone before us
and a hope for those still here,
both of whom are held tight
in God's loving arms.

Contents

prologue: we all grieve 1

floodwaters of grief 27

gushing grief 33

big and frequent drips 63

continued drips 75

the space between 89

the beauty 117

we can heal 147

epilogue: to experience God 167

poetry index 180

Yet I

My heart is broken
yet I rejoice
for it is only
from loving so deep
that grief
can pierce so intense.

Prologue
we all grieve

The death of a loved one changes you.
It changes how you view the world.
It causes a seismic shift.

The world you once knew is different
and forever will be.

Whether you saw it coming or it caught you off guard,
there's nothing you can do to change the fact—
the death of a loved one changes you.

How it changes you?

That's up to you.

Healing Space

Time doesn't heal;
time gives you
the space needed
to heal yourself.

I sit, writing this, under the shade of a tree and watch a white butterfly flutter around me. I've seen many white butterflies as of late. It feels symbolic—like a kiss from heaven.

White Butterflies

the beauty; the purity
floating here and there
fluttering to and fro
reminding me to relax
take it easy
be light; be graceful
enjoy the simplicity
be still; be free

Peace is what I find when I'm in nature.
My pain subsides as I focus on the surrounding beauty.
It's enough to take my breath away.

I continue watching the butterfly flit and flutter against
the pale blue sky. Clouds like stretched taffy linger in the air.

A cardinal flies low and across the yard.

Hymns

The cardinal sings
hymns from Heaven; speaking love
to my broken heart.

A squirrel scampers up a tree and looks back
as if to entice me to a game of chase.

I'll pass.

Sitting in solitude, I enjoy the tranquility.
My mind at ease even as my heart is breaking.

I know healing is a process. And right now, it feels like a…

Slow Drip

Grief is like a slow drip.

drip

drip

People deal with it differently.
differently
differently

What am I supposed to say
when asked "how are you doing?"
doing
doing

My standard reply is "good."
good
good

I know I'll get by.
by
by

The sun will shine again tomorrow.
tomorrow
tomorrow

I choose to believe that's true.
true
true

But for now,
grief feels like a slow drip…

drip

drip

This is my story of loss, grief, and healing.

It started like a gushing flood.
Then the drips began.
Quick at first. And powerful.
But eventually space distanced the drips.

It is within this space there appears a place for healing.
It doesn't happen all at once; it's incremental.

And God met me here—in the midst of my pain.
By being willing to deal, God has been able to heal.

If you picked up this book, you likely have your own story of loss, and though our stories won't be the same, we share a commonality.

We all grieve.
We all lose people we love.
We all ache for what we've lost.

And by sharing our varied experiences,
we begin to understand, we are not alone,
and we will get through.

Foggy Mourn

The fog sitting stale over the rolling hills
after a treacherous rain
mirrors my bleak and muted heart,
still in disbelief that you were taken away.

But hope, buried deep,
knows in time the fog will rise and dissipate;
a day of sunlight will shine once more
though now I sit in my foggy mourn.

My faith clings to God's promise,
that in due time, hope will resurrect
my heart of sorrow into life once again.

floodwaters of grief

For me…

It was sudden. Unexpected.
And the second time to happen this way.

It's a collapsing moment—
when life ends.

The floodwaters of grief open, and there's nothing to stop its flow.
Waves of disbelief and confusion crashed over me.
A fog quickly set in.

Flooding

memories flooding
my mind; remembering you,
a piece of me gone

Separation from the ones you love will always bring heartache and pain. And you never forget where you were when you got the news. It's etched into your heart and mind.

Strong emotions do that.

Our greatest joys and greatest pains etch deeply.
Loss leaves a wound that needs healing.

Glimmer of Hope

As you sit in the darkness
let the tears stream down your face;
let the anger burst forth and release it,
but cling to the glimmer,
cling to the glimmer of light
for it is your hope.

As you wait in the darkness
let time pass by;
grieve for how your life will now be different,
and cling to the glimmer,
cling to the glimmer of light
for it is your hope.

As you stand in the darkness
growing tall in the midst of your pain,
you will find a strength you never knew you had;
so cling to the glimmer,
cling to the glimmer of light
for it is your hope.

As you sit, as you wait, as you stand,
this glimmer of light will become brighter and stronger,
engulfing the darkness until the light fully shines over you again.

But until then,
cling to the glimmer,
cling to the glimmer of light
for it is your hope.

gushing grief

I don't have much clarity of those first forty-eight hours. It seemed the world was moving, but I was standing still—stuck in an automaton state of incomprehension. I tried to make it make sense, but I couldn't formulate any words.

Jumbled and trapped fragments of thought felt like a prison between my ears. As I climbed into bed that second night, what came to mind was King David crying out to God in so many prayers recorded in the Psalms. I imagined some were unintelligible utterings and groanings. That too was my struggle, until a single thought came as a coherent prayer.

Language of Tears

when grief overwhelms
and you have no words
God hears the language
of your heartfelt tears

Let me rewind a bit for context:

My Aunt Beck was twenty when I was born, and I was the apple of her eye. Well, maybe I'm being a bit generous, but we definitely had a special bond.

Growing up, I spent Thursday nights and Fridays with her building memories. The month before I turned five, she got married. Being the flower girl, I had a dress similar to hers and was quite excited for our big day. I felt like a princess, and she looked like a queen. But during the ceremony, my little mind started connecting the dots. This new Uncle Steve would be taking my Aunt Becky far, far away. As my cheery disposition dissolved into tears, I was removed from the ceremony.

I saw her a couple times each year and was able to adjust. Then, when I was eleven, my immediate family moved from Oklahoma to Michigan, and we were again living near one another. It wasn't the fifteen minute drive we once had, but it sure beat the fifteen hour drive. Life was good.

As I entered adulthood, we stayed close and felt more like sisters and friends. Life without her never crossed my mind. So when that gushing flood of unexpected grief broke open, I felt like that little girl who needed to be removed from the ceremony. But this time, my aunt moved to a place I wouldn't be able to visit.

I desperately wanted to hear her voice—to hear her tell me it'd be okay.

The silence was deafening.

In the midst of the upheaval, my usual outlet of expression was dammed. I floundered in my ocean of emotion—denial crashing upon reality.

As I gathered pictures for her memorial service, I was looking for a very specific one.

Where would it be?

Tossing photo albums onto my bed, only one flipped open. And there it was—my little hands cupping her beautiful face.

It felt as if she reached down from Heaven and opened it herself.
I was overwhelmed, and the thought came…

She'll speak differently now, but she'll still be with me.

With that impression on my heart,
I walked to my desk and sat down.

The following words flowed
as if guided by her love.

Words from Heaven

God welcomed me Home—into His loving arms,
and I'm in perfect peace for now I see His bigger picture.

But I know you're hurting; I see you grieving and in pain.
I'm watching you from the heavens, and I come to you as you cry.

Feel me wrap my arms around you as I pull and hold you close.
The warmth you feel against your skin is my touch.
The wind sweeping by are whispers, "I love you."

My spirit talks to yours
to remind you I'm still here
and always will be.

So let's sit awhile in the quiet;
allow yourself to be aware of me.

I'll now talk to you in different ways.
You'll know it's me from the message,
a little something special just for you.

Keep the faith, hope, and love strong
for that is our deepest connection.
They are the legacy of eternal truth.

Just as God guides us on earth to touch others,
He guides us in Heaven to do the same.
You may even entertain me
as an angel one day.

God is so gracious, and His love endures.
As part of this heavenly realm, I now know beauty everlasting.

One day we'll welcome you here with arms open wide.
Until then, every time the wind blows, hear me whisper
"I love you—always have, always do, always will."

That first weekend, I set out on the three-hour drive to her home. My heart ached to be with her family, which had grown over the years to include four sons and now three daughters-in-law and five grandsons.

I've always enjoyed long drives on open roads. The silence and stillness allows my mind to wonder, ponder, and process—creating an open and receptive state of being.

Pulling onto the highway, I headed east. Dark clouds gathered in the distance, matching the heaviness of my heart. An hour into the drive, I merged southbound. Light was breaking through, and I felt my aunt whisper, "be strong; I love you!"

Storms of Life

I saw the storm clouds rolling in,
across the horizon—dark and gray.
But it was the direction I had to go
to get home.

My only option was to be wise,
be safe, be prepared the best I could.

Storms are a part of life's journey.
Sometimes they're just sprinkles.

Sometimes they're so rough
you don't know how you'll make it through.

Sometimes you just have to find a place to shelter in its midst.
Instead of passing through the storm, let the storm pass over you.

But rest and know these storms won't last forever.
A ray of light is on the other side, preparing to break through.
No storm can handle the powerful force of light's intention.

In time, the sun will shine in all its glorious hues,
and you'll be stronger having overcome the storm.

Storms of life are inevitable.
How you handle them—that's up to you.

God is always speaking—always revealing Himself.

But I have to have spiritual eyes to see and spiritual ears to hear the language of Heaven. This truth expands more each day I live seeking awareness.

Continuing on the drive, I saw a large, black bird flying high with three smaller birds following. *A momma and her boys,* I mused. *If only it had been four.*

A short bit down the road, I saw a bird sitting on a wire all by itself when another bird swooped in, and they flew off together—as if they were both going back to momma. One letting the other know, "you're never alone; we're in this together."

Different

When we lose someone we love
be patient with one another.

Each grieves and processes differently.
No right and no wrong;
just different.

Honor your loved ones
by accepting these differences.

Everyone will grieve in their own way,
and in their own time,
as you do the same.

Further down the road, I saw a large, black bird flying high, by itself. I smiled, thinking of my aunt flying high, up toward Heaven.

My mind shifted to a poem I had written a few weeks prior.

Black Wings

soaring and circling
spreading and gliding
across the cotton ball clouds
and softly fading blue sky

like hope living, breathing life

reminding me to look up,
even when I'm falling

Falls are an inevitable part of life's journey. Sometimes they come from our own doing; sometimes they come from beyond our control.

However they come, the risk of falling remains, so perspective is key.

What will I do? Where will I focus? How will I respond?

My own words brought comfort—*look up, even when I'm falling.* Wisdom I know deep down but don't always recall in the moment of a restless and wounded mind. Yet, truth resonates on a deep soul and spirit level.

Within truth, peace is found. From peace, love overflows. In the overflow, joy springs eternal. This is the living, breathing, eternal hope that empowers one to rise again. We are created to be victorious—more than conquerors, overcomers in this life.

Driving alone that first Sunday, to her small country church, the falling rain reminded me of her.

Almost fifteen years prior, we'd driven together down a similar country road. I, in the passenger seat, staring out the window as clouds released thick droplets back to earth.

Her youngest brother, Tom, who was just a few years older than me, had moved to Heaven unexpectedly.

"I think God's crying with our family," I softly stated. "He's sad for our pain."

She nodded in agreement. Her eyes never leaving the road.

We continued. Silence speaking. Tears gathering. Emotion releasing from heavy hearts.

Now, here I was, once again—a dark sky with a deluge of rain pouring onto my windshield. I stopped in the middle of the road, near the railroad crossing she always warned me about.

Staring in silence my heart heard her say, "I was thinking the same."

Without

the pelting of rain
mirrors the loss in my heart;
alone without you

My poetry blog became a little inconsistent during this time, but I did manage to post some sunset pictures I'd taken the previous month.

I like sunsets. They're hopeful.

The sun rises; the sun falls—all to do it over again the next day, and the next, and the next…

Sunsetting Nights

As the sun does set
and says good-night,
so I too, with all my might,
close my eyes and dream tonight
of possibilities and new insight.

The post was unbeknownst to my mom, and the next day she sent me a short video montage her phone automatically compiles from her images. It opened on a picture of my aunt with the sun setting behind her. My heart smiled. *Words from Heaven.*

The following Saturday was her memorial—a beautiful mix of tears and laughter. But as people gathered after the service, I found it hard to sit and talk with anyone. This wasn't my norm. Even in loss, I've always appreciated seeing and visiting with extended family. But this time was different. I pushed myself to be social, but my heart only wanted to be around her immediate family or left alone.

As the noise clamored in the crowded fellowship hall, I made my escape to the outside. The wind was strong, blowing my hair wildly across my face. When I reached the far side of the parsonage, I leaned against the exterior wall and released a big breath of appreciation for the quiet. The wind calmed, and I snickered. *Beck was being quite adamant to show me she was still here.*

> ...every time the wind blows, hear me whisper
> "I love you—always have, always do, always will."

With eyes closed, I smiled toward the sun and felt the warmth of her love. It was then I realized why this memorial was so hard. My heart was still looking for her. She had always been a constant source of strength and love. When she was around, it was as if an invisible tether held us together. But now that tether had no weight, and I felt aimlessly adrift.

Come Into My Arms

there's a hole
something missing
you're trying to fill
come into My arms

bring your void
bring your emptiness
only I can satisfy
come into My arms

let me hold you
let me cover you
let me love you
come into My arms

back into wholeness
back into Oneness
with Me
come into My arms

like a blanket of warmth
covering you tight
feel My peace
come into My arms

Family went their way by Sunday, but I stayed a bit longer.

I was glad I could, yet I wasn't. We can have such oppositional feelings at times. But in this tension, we have opportunity for discovery.

Being alone in her house, I walked around taking it all in. It felt empty. It felt different. And my heart hurt. I couldn't recall ever being in her home without her.

She had inspirational and scripture wall art throughout. With a grin, I wondered if Hobby Lobby's stock price would go down now that she was gone.

Wanting to remember the words that meant something to her, I started snapping pictures. In the living room, a pillow with the phrase—it's so good to be home—stood out. *How appropriate, I thought. She is truly Home—surrounded and One with love, peace, and joy eternal.*

Sitting in her chair, I saw my poetry collection *God is so much more* atop a basket of books. She had been the first person for a lot of things in my life, including the first person to whom I gave an inscribed copy.

I picked it up and opened it to the bookmarked page—
just what I needed to hear. *More words from Heaven.*

Dry

When the well runs dry,
and hope feels empty and bare,
God's love will find you.

In the midst of my sadness, in the midst of my confusion, I chose to trust in God's unfailing love. I chose to trust that His peace would deepen within my heart and mind, etching permanence.

It can be a process to remember that God always is, always was, and always will be here with me. But it's true.

And though I felt lost, God's love had already found me.
All I needed was to claim that truth down from the heavens.

Always Found

God meets me where I am.
God gives me what I need.
God is always here,
though sometimes I don't see.

Sometimes I don't feel Him.
My faith, at times, runs thin.
But when I'm sinking deep in pain
I still call on Him.

Sometimes it's in my anger.
Sometimes it's through my tears.
Yet I have always found
He holds me close and pulls me near.

Like a child who throws a tantrum
or one who's hurt and softly cries,
God holds me in my pain
and looks into my eyes.

His presence brings me comfort.
When I slow down I clearly see.
My God is everywhere.
His love surrounding me.

big and frequent drips

The big and frequent drips felt after losing someone can take many forms. Today, it felt as if I'd fallen into a canyon—dark, lonely, and cold. Staying here in the depths doesn't seem so bad. I could get used to this—just numbing myself from reality. The world offers plenty of ways to do so. But I know deep down, I'm not looking for a temporary band-aid. I desire healing.

Hold On

I'm sinking,
and sinking fast.
Barely keeping
my head above water.

A disappearance
would ease my pain.
But it would ripple more pain
onto those who are already hurting.

So I thrash and gasp
my energy diminishing as I tread.
Waves of emotion continue
to crash over my head.

"Hold on; hold on a little longer,"
I hear a soft whisper within.
"Help is on its way."

Though I didn't know where I'd find the strength to climb out of that deep canyon of grief, I found a way. Because God always makes a way. He is the way. And when you choose to deal, His strength becomes yours.

To Believe

All things are possible
when you choose
to believe.

That's the beauty
of faith,
and the power
of moving
mountains.

The intermingling of grief and healing can feel like white water rafting. The twists and turns, the ups and downs. It requires flexibility as you navigate.

Rapids

I hear the rapids
before we take the turn.

My heart beats faster
as the calm waters disappear.

The river narrows;
rugged rocks draw near.

This is what we've been waiting for.

Water splashing;
we listen to the guide,
eventually arriving
on the other side.

Back to calm waters.

My heart slows and all can rest;
feeling triumphant though soaking wet.

We faced our challenge—we overcame;
a lot like life so isn't it a shame
when we see resistance and call it a foe,
maybe it's just life helping us grow.

Loss is definitely not a checklist item. It's an emotionally draining and hard path to walk. I'm reminded of wise words my mom has said regarding tough times, "sometimes you have to choose your hard."

I can have short-term relief followed by long-term pain.

OR

I can have short-term pain followed by long-term relief.

When I looked at it that way, it was quite simple, but that didn't mean it would be easy.

As the year progressed, I had a few arguments with my tear-streaked face in the mirror. "This dealing sucks! It's not worth it!" My dripping nose kept me walking back to the bathroom, past my reflection—where I could see my weariness growing, slowly displacing my pent up anger and hurt.

It was here, in my weakness and exhaustion, I leaned into God. And in God, I found my rest.

Mountaintop View

As the fog settles,
I hunker in the Rock and find my refuge.

When the fog lifts,
I stand on the Rock and find my strength.

For under the shining sun, I see new heights;
greater understanding has been revealed.

Will I have feet that float like a feather
or am I wearing concrete boots?

The latter keeps me in the refuge of safety,
but I seek the mountaintop view.

Up is the only Way.

Though I was determined to venture to the mountaintop, there were many tumbles along the way. At first, I didn't realize that would be the case.

With the busyness of life, I'd set grief aside on an intellectual level, but emotions clung tight. When I forgot to deal with my thoughts, the emotions constricted, tighter and tighter, until they burst into overwhelming drips—falling fast and hard.

A quarter up the mountain, weak and weary, was my first tumble. Halfway up, I fell again—harder. Three quarters of the way up, light was illuminating brightly.

"Ah, I'm there!"

But before I knew it, I whipped all the way back to the bottom—to what felt like an even deeper despair.

"How is this even possible? I've been so intentional to deal!"

As I lay in my frustration, heartache pulsating to my core, I realized…

Even in these depths, God is still with me.

Together

when I was broken
when I was weak
when I was weary

it was here
that I found God

in my deepest valley
the only perspective remaining
was to look up

I saw the sun casting rays across treetops
the mountains spread out like arms open wide
my feet stood firm on the earth's foundation
as the wind sung a song of wisdom

carry on my child; I am the Way
rest in Me, every day
We'll get through this together
you can handle any weather
listen close and trust what I say

continued drips

I didn't want loss to overtake me.

I wanted it to shape me, mold me, transform me in a beautiful way. But it didn't always feel that would be the case.

We often don't realize the emotions we're suppressing to get through a situation or through the day. We sweep them under the rug, either to deal with them later or to flat-out ignore them. Whatever the reason, doing so can be detrimental to ourselves and our relationships.

Six weeks in, the sadness and grief that had been grinding in my mind came to a pinnacle. It felt claustrophobic, and I knew I needed space.

Jumping in my car, I drove the highway in silence. Well, maybe I screamed a few times. It may seem juvenile, but I've found it to be a beneficial outlet. By releasing pent up emotion, my thinking clears. It was here, in this release, the stages of grief came to mind.

With the initial **loss,** I was smacked with a gush of fierce water. I didn't want to deal with the force, so I tried to turn it off through **denial**. But the big and frequent drips remained, and I got **angry**. I questioned; I asked why; I **bargained** for what other outcomes might have changed the situation. At times, I felt like throwing in the sopping, wet towel and giving up on hope; a numbed-out, **depressive** state seemed appealing. I certainly had my moments.

But I reminded myself that's all part of the process—a process that takes time—a process that eventually leads to **acceptance**.

Whirlwind

When emotions run so deep
we can't find the words to say,
it's like rain caught in a whirlwind.

May we release these emotions as tears
allowing the cleanse to take shape;
emotions puddling after the storm.

Then sifting through the havoc,
we organize our thoughts into words,
albeit still murky.

This process of clean-up and re-setting
is how we create meaning from feeling
so we can now formulate the words to say.

Like all emotions, anger is nothing more than an alert to get our attention—it tells us something is out of alignment. On the highway drive, anger benefited me greatly as it was the catalyst for remembering the stages of grief. These stages are normal—to be expected and accepted—if one wants to heal.

Beauty of Tears

when words can't express what we feel
tears take their place
whether in sorrow or joy
it's an expression from the heart
when the mind is at a loss

healing waters arise
to set free the emotion building within
let the waters escape; don't dam them

it's a process of beauty
it's a process of healing
it's a process to behold

relax and release
for when the tears have run free
the calm will return
and lighter you will be

Once anger had my attention, I had a choice...

Capture my thinking and transform it into a beneficial perspective.

OR

Let my thoughts run rampant—creating havoc in my mind and overflowing my life with ill action.

I chose the prior—to welcome anger with open arms and ask...

"What's at the root of this anger?"

"What might I learn about myself if I sit still with this anger?"

"How might my perspective change if I sit still with this anger?"

The way I choose to deal with my emotions, as I journey through loss, will greatly impact my healing.

Sit Awhile

Come friend, sit awhile,
and tell me what's on your mind.

I won't judge;
I'm here to listen.
I want to show my support;
I want you to know I care.

Just think what our ill emotions might reveal
if we were as gentle and compassionate with them
as we are toward a dear friend.

Come emotions, sit awhile,
and tell me what's on your mind?

God's Whisper

to hear the gentle whisper
the storm within must calm
be still; be at peace

it is here you hear
empty yourself of all the ills
breathe in God's goodness
let it settle over you
like a soft breeze on a warm day

an oasis of beauty
within each of us
awaiting discovery
claim residence

the serene within grows
as you cultivate the space
expanding God's peace
into every fiber of your being
creating balance and unity
from inside, out

Eleven months in, my birthday arrived. I love celebrating birthdays. They serve as a reminder to just how beautiful and joyous the gift of life truly is.

But two days later, I overreacted to a minor inconvenience—this surprised me. As I sat in stillness that evening, I intended to count my blessings, but my mind kept wandering.

Then it hit me…

Beck's grandson, Wade, has a birthday the day before mine. He turned six this year, and I was excited to celebrate with her crew. After pulling up to the house, I got out and crossed the spot where she had hugged me and wished me happy birthday the year before. She was always the first to do that—it was a competition for her. But now, the game would no longer be played. Keeping that moment to myself, I entered the house with hugs and a smile.

This was one of those continued drips, like a small tumble after arriving on the mountaintop. It's understandable to put your feelings aside. Not all times are appropriate to deal. But if you forget to deal—intentionally or not—they will come back to deal with you.

The Cove

Recessed along the shore.
Waves lapping where the cliffs meet sand.

The cove sits.

Tranquil.
Dark inside.
Sounds echo.

Reverberating nature's song.
The world beyond dances to life.
As I float in solitude and contemplation.
Darkness can be instrumental for awakening awareness.

the
*space
between*

For me...

Grief is private.
Grief is personal.

And it reminds me a lot of spirituality.

I can be with others along the way.
I can share what I'm learning, but it's intimate.
There's a necessity for honesty, authenticity, and vulnerability.

When I air my hurts and lay them before God, I feel better.

For All Who Are Lost

God is here
to take the beating
you throw upon Him,
to take the words
when you lash out,
to take the brunt
of all your anger
because He wants you
to seek Him out.

He won't step away
no matter your offenses.
He won't turn His back,
He'll stay steadfast.
He wants to protect you
and take your burden.
He wants to hold you
for love will outlast.

All the confusion,
the hurt and the heartache,
all the pain and silence
when asking why.

There are not always answers
our minds can fathom
on this side of eternity's sky.

So when you're broken and beaten
no strength to go on,
tears welling inside
like a dam breaking at dawn,
surrender your burdens
place them at the cross,
this is the place
for all who are lost.

You can experience a peace
deep down inside
when you come and find rest
and choose not to hide,
for God knows your story
you're part of the Divine—
a beautiful, wanted, and loved child,
a humanly, heavenly, almighty sign.

Grief also reminds me of spirituality because the two have been so intertwined in my life. Losses—big and small—have provided me the opportunity to delve deeper into my faith or to turn from it.

Over and over again, I've chosen the former because over and over again, God has proven Himself faithful. He is bigger than any problem life throws my way, and He is bigger than any feeling I throw His way.

I trust in His unconditional love. Even when acting immaturely, my spirit knows He desires to hold me tight.

Wrestling with God

In my hardest losses,
I've wrestled with God
trying to make sense of it all.

I've screamed; I've kicked.
I've had quite the tantrums
like a toddler not getting her way.

But when my energy fades
I'm left weary and broken,
and that's right where I need to be.
For God never leaves; He's always here
loving and holding me.

When I wrestle with God
instead of running away
our relationship has gone much deeper.
He's always the same, has been, and will be,
forever He is my keeper.

By being raw and honest with God, I exposed everything…

my fury
my frustration
my pain
my hurt
my brokenness
my vulnerability

It was in this bare state, I was left with no cover—no place to hide. He had me exactly where He wanted me. I was at His mercy.

And I discovered…

Only God

You.
Love.
Me.
No matter
my past.
No matter
my present.
No matter
my future.
Pure love.
Is.
Your love.
I can't escape.
I don't want to escape.
I melt into
You.
Love.
Me.

I began to understand, on a deeper level, my Oneness with God. My heart began beating with His, to the rhythm of Heaven's music.

Within these beats—in this sacred space—I began to discover the fullness of God and His love—a love so much greater than my mind can intellectually grasp.

Love Like Water

If My love for you were water
all the oceans of this world
would pale in comparison
to the floods that would
cover the earth.

From the moment we take our first breath, God is revealing Himself—His depths, His fullness—it's a beautiful and never-ending process, unfolding each day, whether we recognize it or not. Like the oxygen we breath, God is the life force within our lungs.

When we lean into Him and His love, we grow like a seed into a mature tree—roots form, deep and strong—below the surface, in the dark. From above—the sun, the water, the nutrients—all feed the soil, providing the atmosphere for growth. And when the time is right, the seedling bursts forth as a small bloom, its be-coming presents itself—potential manifesting.

In this growth, my understanding deepens, revealing more of who God is within me, who I am in Him, and our union and ever-expanding Oneness—this is His truth, this is His peace—a peace that passes all understanding.

The Peace that Transcends

The paradox of having peace in chaos
is the ability to transcend your situation.

This peace is found when
you lift your eyes above
and focus on the Peace-maker.

For God's peace transcends explanation.

It's not a fact; it's not a feeling.
It's the presence of the living God
inundating your being,
unifying your soul
back as One.

The ability to have peace in chaos
comes from grounding yourself
in the truth of God, and
who God says you are.

You are worthy; you are loved.

Be still; be One.

When the soul gets wounded, such as with loss, it creates opportunity for spirituality to awaken—to transcend beyond religion to relationship, to exchange formality for authenticity, to see through the illusion of separation to the truth of Oneness—this is Kingdom living.

In a world that offers band-aid solutions, God offers something different—what God offers is real. Regardless of what I feel moment-by-moment, truth remains steadfast. He is my Rock, my firm foundation, in all things and at all times.

His love draws me in, His peace holds me tight, and I find rest knowing my joy will come once again. Ease will displace my grief-laden emotions. And like all wounds tended to, my soul will be mended and healed. Grief is not part of my identity—it's not who I am. It's only alerting me to the fact that I must deal with what I feel if I desire to heal.

This intermingling of grief and healing is part of the process because they're two sides of the same coin—the coin of this earthly experience.

On which side do I choose to focus?

Healing OR *Grief*

When Lost

That which makes life so beautiful,
when lost, is what makes life so hard.

Coming to accept this truth,
that you can't have one without the other,
produces a transformation within.

Creating proper perspective and understanding;
they are two sides of the same coin.

Learn to appreciate and love deeply
yet hold with open hands,
for a time will come when you need
to release and let go.

This is the balance of life.

Lean into these feelings of joy and sorrow;
they are both needed to fully comprehend.

When I started working on this book, I referenced it as my grief book. Then one day it hit me—by using that name I was allowing grief to maintain a hold over me. In that moment, I decided this was no longer my grief book; this was my healing book.

This is my story of overcoming.

Though Beck's body may rest as dust, her soul and spirit are eternal. She has arisen into new life—this is Spirit reality. She exchanged this earthly experience of illusory duality for the realm of truth—Oneness—she is now alive, more than ever.

And she doesn't want me to journey through life carrying the burden of a grief-laden grave. With God by her side, they are calling me into the abundant life—to walk this earth in the authority and power of Christ's death and resurrection, each and every day.

> "Keep the faith, hope, and love strong
> for that is our deepest connection.
> They are the legacy of eternal truth."

I can be healed. I can overcome. I am created to rise again.

We are all called to new life—a resurrected life of Kingdom living—a life of love, peace, and joy in this present moment.

It is all for us—all we have is now.

Death can't keep me in the ground.

Each Day

Each day I will count my blessings
even if the skies turn gray.
I will hold my head toward Heaven
and this is what I'll say,

"You've walked with me in sunshine;
You've carried me through the storms.
No matter what's before me
I choose to be transformed.

My character is developing
as I continue to walk in Your ways.
Your light brightens my path
guiding all of my days.

Your presence is my peace.
Your love holds me tight.
I have joy in my heart
every day, every night.

That doesn't mean life is perfect;
it just means I choose to see
the perfection of Your goodness
for that changes me."

So each day I count my blessings
even when the skies turn gray.
I am grateful to be Your child;
I choose Your Life, Your Truth, Your Way.

Knowing this wisdom, I would think I'd be better at letting go. But too often, I still cling to my burdens. As if in letting go, I'll lose a part of myself. But that's not true.

The burden of loss is not who I am. I don't want to, nor do I have to, identify that way. Loss and ill emotions will weigh me down. But each day I practice releasing and letting go, I get better.

Practice is always how we get better. Healthy habits are formed through intention and repetition. As I lean into God and His ways, this truth deepens within me.

We are meant to be whole; we are meant to be One. And God is here to compassionately put our broken pieces back together, to heal our wounds, making us stronger and more beautiful than before.

This is the beauty of His sustaining grace—
overflowing abundant and free,
to any and all who wish to receive.

The Book

Wandering.
Aimless.
I enter.

Smelling the must of vintage books
vertically-lined across the shelves,
some stacked low upon the floor.

Broken.
Searching.
Trying to find my way.

Filling the void
with what others say.

An emptiness aches within.
I struggle to find satisfaction.

Then I pick up one of the books,
used and faded like me,
pages crumpled and torn.

The underlined draws my attention.
<u>God's grace is sufficient.</u>

I ruminate,
for even me?

Further down the page my finger glides
when I notice tiny handwriting along the side.

I squint my eyes so I can see;
someone has written

"Yes, for even me!"

A journal sat on my bookshelf—one I had picked up at the first of the year but had not yet used. Now, it seemed the time was right.

Grabbing it, I smiled.

Imprinted near the four corners were watercolor flowers and in the bright, white center, the words…

"We Got This"

Ah, touché!

With God

With God
it's always "We"
for I'm never alone.

He's always by my side;
every minute, every day.

Anything I face,
We got this.

The same week Beck exchanged earth for Heaven, my design contract of three years came to an end. I had known for a couple weeks it would be concluding—that's how design contracts work—so I planned to enjoy some extra time off visiting her as I lined up my next contract.

At first, it felt like a blessing. I didn't have to juggle priorities and was able to dedicate my time to what mattered most—ensuring her memorial service was beautiful. But once the busyness slowed, reality appeared on my doorstep with a jolting halt. I had nowhere to go and nothing to do. My life felt in shambles.

In the summer of 2019, I had moved to New York City from Fort Worth, Texas. Within three months, I was on a design contract, had an Upper East Side apartment, was watching on and off Broadway shows every week, and was getting my fix of creative classes and neighborhood exploration. The city was abuzz, and so was I.

Then spring 2020 hit. Lockdowns were enforced. Censorship of dissenting voices was prevalent. And by summer, violence was rising. The *anything is possible* energy that drew me to the city was displaced with surreal eeriness followed by unsettling vibes.

I've moved a lot in my adult life, but always at my choosing. This time, it felt like the rug had been pulled out from under my feet. Refusing to be treated like a prisoner in my own neighborhood, I chose to leave.

This period of transition carried its own bag of emotions.

A part of me enjoys the *who knows what's next* excitement, and the other part prefers creating a plan for whatever that *who knows what* might be.

Since I was able to work remotely, I split time with family in Michigan and headed to sunshiny Florida during the coldest months. Having lived in Florida before, I figured it would become my permanent location, but God had different plans.

I began appreciating each season for its fullness instead of just desiring the heat of summer. It was fun to be near family, reconnect with old friends, and make new ones. As God shifted my heart, I eventually knew Michigan was where I would stay and was eager to tell Beck, knowing how excited she'd be. But I never got the chance.

So here I was, not only having lost her, but also so much loss of expectation. I gave myself a month to sit in the ashes of my grief and try to make sense of it all. When the month was up, I'd get back to life—connect with recruiters, connect with friends, and find my groove. That's exactly what I did.

As I made plans and put things in the hopper, I didn't realize the loss and pain I was suppressing. I thought I was doing quite well. But the big and frequent drips made me realize how hard it is to start again, especially when I had so little to go back to.

Things weren't aligning on the job front when I felt God say...

"Don't look for a contract."
"Yeah, but..."

"Just be with Me."
"Um, okay."

The relief I felt upon making that decision assured me I was doing the right thing. So, I spent the next month mostly in solitude with God. I called it my *Tranquility Bay* experience. A part of me loved it, and a part of me felt foolish. But I wouldn't change it, for this solitary time changed me.

Be-coming

*Be always coming
before the Lord.*

You're a different person
for having sat at My feet.
You're a different person
for having prayed.

For time with Me
is about transforming you
back into My likeness,
before Our separation.

I Am who I Am
and together
We are
One.

the beauty

Eventually, the space between the drips increases.

And there, within this space, resides the beauty—the opportunity to transform a grieving heart into a heart of wholeness. That doesn't mean the scar no longer exists; it means I'm no longer bleeding out, lost in my grief.

I envision my aunt looking down from Heaven with a smile, proud of the healing transformation taking place within my soul and spirit. I know she desires me to be at peace, to act with love, and to live in joy—for this is the abundant life.

Throne of Healing

Healing is from God
because wholeness is of God.

We are created to be One.

In this truth, we find peace,
and from peace, love overflows.
This union creates joy.

Soul and Spirit becoming One.
Single-minded.

The Kingdom of God is within.
The Kingdom of Heaven is among.

The Throne of Healing is open to all.
The Way. The Truth. The Life.

Choose to believe
for your faith heals you.

By surrendering to God's healing power,
I am able, in the most beautiful way, to honor Beck—
to carry on her legacy and to keep her a part of me.

Souvenir

Faith, hope, and love are here,
and like a treasured souvenir,
I can carry them with me
everywhere I go.

Legacy

A tree buds
new life grows.

Leaves flourish
thick and green.

Beauty peaks
sunset colors.

As leaves fall,
nutrients are absorbed
preparing for the next season.

Much like a legacy,
laying a foundation
for the next generation.

Beauty in the Barren

As a tree loses its leaves,
I see beauty in the barrenness
knowing it's a season that will lead to rebirth.

Too often we resist the natural process
of shedding the old to allow for the new;
resistance arrests our growth and development.

Trust that which fades away was meant to go;
trust it's all for your best.

Rest in knowing you don't have to understand
to release and let go; sadness is okay,
but don't cling to it as an anchor
if you want to move forward and heal.

Let the tears of expression flow;
let them wash over you
breaking the dams of emotional resistance.

Open yourself to Heaven's healing power.
Trust that resurrection makes all things new.
Learn to see beauty in the barren.

Four and a half months in, the holiday season arrived.

Loss in the Holidays

Dealing with loss in the holiday season
leaves me adrift in a sea of joy and grief.

Wanting to celebrate the beauty,
but sadness striking as someone's missing.
Waves of joy and waves of grief
crash one onto the other.

Mixed emotions are to be expected
and accepted as part of the process.

In time, these waves of joy will lengthen
and these waves of grief will shorten,
but until then I rest in remembering
the memories and emotions of it all.

The one I love, the one I dearly miss
is always with me for where love is,
love was, love always will be.

I understand love because God first loved me.
I feel love because it's alive in this season;
I am this love when I give to another.

My loved one now sings with the angels.
Christ was born to redeem all of creation;
this truth brings comfort in the midst of my loss.

Prince of Peace; Wonderful Counselor.
God is all I need; He'll get me through.

In His presence, in His love, I find my rest, I celebrate.
Hark the herald angels sing, glory to the newborn King.

He makes all things new;
death is not the end; eternity awaits.

Those with eyes, let him see.
Those with ears, let him hear.

Breaking Through

Snow falling softly
against a gray, cloudy sky
invoking feelings of sadness and loss.

I close my eyes
and see my loved one
treasured and cherished,
held in my heart.

Love warms me.

I open my eyes
and see snow falling softly
against a gray, cloudy sky
now invoking feelings of hope,
for with faith I see differently.

I choose to see the light beyond the gray clouds;
faith, hope, and love rest on the horizon,
breaking through.

This Holiday Scene

Diamonds dance across the ground
reflecting the starlit sky.
A winter chill in the air
as strangers pass on by.

I'm sitting on a wooden bench
enjoying this holiday scene.
Taking it all in,
the beauty is serene.

The smell of sappy firs,
carols echoing nearby,
cherished memories in my heart,
a teardrop in my eye.

I've always been excited to kick off a new year, enthralled with anticipation of what may come. It's a necessity—one year drawing to a close, allowing the next to begin—as when winter fades into spring's welcoming warmth.

I wanted my perspective to match these transitioning seasons. So that's what I chose. I trusted my healing would continue to displace my grief. Though, at times, it felt slow.

Transitioning Seasons

into Spring.
The tombs of winter's gloom having melded into wombs;
awakening a new season
filled with hope, potential, and possibilities
which will lead us...

into Summer.
Brightly lit sun and expansive skies;
we frolic and play in the fullness of each day.
Growing and becoming
that for which the seed within was planted
which will lead us...

into Fall.
A time of quieting and contemplation
to meditate on that which was, is, and is to come.
A time of deep gratitude and releasing
of the things that need to go
which will lead us...

into Winter.
A time of dormancy, a waiting state,
a resting until the conditions are right;
developing within, from tombs to wombs.
Rebirth comes on the other side
which will lead us...

These seasons are eternal.
These seasons are perishable.
These seasons are spiritual.
These seasons are physical.
These seasons are a lifetime.
These seasons are a day.
These seasons are now.
These seasons have been and will be.

Recognize the beauty of these seasons.
Recognize the beauty of these transitions.
Recognize the beauty that all is for you.

From tombs of barrenness to wombs of birth;
awaken to the full measure of Life.

Placed before me is a life of hope and healing or the tomb of loss and grief. The latter, being a natural part of the journey, had served its purpose, and its season was coming to an end. Death could no longer hold me in the ground. I intentionally chose to re-create, to seek the beautiful life of hope and healing.

Blessed Are They

There are a lot of beliefs about God,
but this I know to be true...

God is love.
God is goodness.
God is patience.
God is kindness.
God is gentleness.
God is compassion.
God is forgiveness.
God is all the beauty of the world.

When we seek wholeness, we will find Oneness;
and when God flows through us...

Love flows through us.
Goodness flows through us.
Patience flows through us.
Kindness flows through us.
Gentleness flows through us.
Compassion flows through us.
Forgiveness flows through us.
All the beauty of the world flows through us.

For as One...

We are love.
We are goodness.
We are patience.
We are kindness.
We are gentleness.
We are compassion.
We are forgiveness.
We are all the beauty of the world.

This is Spirit reality transcending the physical.
The re-becoming; the re-union with God.

Revelation leads to revolution.
A transformation of the mind;
battlefields becoming gardens.

Thy kingdom come, Thy will be done
on earth as it is in heaven.

When the physical has been pricked,
the spiritual awakens from its deep slumber.

The Kingdom of God is within.
The Kingdom of Heaven is here, now.

Always has been, always will be.
Since the beginning of time 'til the end.

Come out of the tombs,
rise from the graves;
you were created to live
a resurrected life.

The veil has been torn.
God is in us and among us.
Listen close and hear Him say…

"This is My way, walk in it;
blessed are they."

Love Brings You Home

The one true love
your heart cries out for
is the Master Artist,
whose image you bear.

If you are still, you'll feel
this longing for Oneness.
Too often we fill this longing
with worldly pleasures,
but they won't satisfy.

The ache that burns deep down,
the part you're missing,
that disconnect,
it's separation from the One.

The longing is beautiful tho,
for it's the hole—that missing piece
in every soul—that pulls you toward Home.

Desiring to be back in the hands
of the Master Artist,
Who has always been here,
calling you by name.

Life may take you to unexpected places,
but Love brings you Home.
Back into Oneness.
Love makes you whole.

By intentionally leaning into God and resting in Him, I found the healing balm for my wounded heart.

In this place of peaceful Oneness, I knew His radiance would shine within me, bright like diamonds.

Be a Diamond

The sun came out
lighting the dreary sky;
the snow melted in its warmth,
and gathered at the corner of the porch roof,
dazzling like diamonds, and falling
as individual drips onto the earth.
So it is when we allow God to shine in us and through us;
we dazzle and reflect His goodness and beauty
throughout all creation.

we can
heal

Embrace

those we love
are always near
for our hearts
are intertwined
forever lasting
from always
to eternity
linked in love
bonded infinity
loss is temporal
an illusion of sorts
union is heavenly
reality of truth
love is the way
abundant living
here and now
close your eyes
open your vision
embrace pure
unconditional love
a love that is
patient and kind
always protecting
hoping and persevering
a love that never fails

When faced with loss, we'll never be the same because we're not supposed to be. We are to be transformed each and every day. I trust my sorrow will turn to joy, for I trust God makes all things new. I trust God comforts the brokenhearted.

There were mornings I woke up sad, mornings I woke up apathetic, mornings I woke up depressed, but I chose to carry on—believing that eventually my joy would come. Believing that my feelings would catch up to my faith and God's truth would breathe life into my soul once again.

Time is what made these slow drips so beautiful, for they were gifts from God—providing me opportunity to transform my perspective.

Over time, I realized I control the speed at which the water flows. No longer are there unexpected outbursts of grief and sadness. Though I may still feel these emotions, I'm able to adjust my perspective, and in doing so, my understanding deepens, transforming my heart and mind into closer relationship with God.

Very early on, I felt the need to document this journey.

Having been through an unexpected loss before, I knew how much it had transformed me into the person I am today.

That knowledge helped me lean into my pain and sorrow as if I were working through a diagnosis as both physician and patient. Through observation and awareness, I felt God deepening my understanding and expanding it with revelation.

Still, I waned back and forth as I worked to turn my scribbled notes into this book. A part of me preferring to stay private, but the Voice within prompting me to share. I shelved it a few times. Maybe I started too early and still had too much grief to work through. Or maybe that was just part of the process.

Each time I re-visited my writings, I was able to re-view and re-assess my thoughts, beliefs, and feelings. By holding them up to observation, I could see God transforming my heart and mind in real time.

Then, around month nine, something shifted. As I organized my thoughts and began typing them into articulated paragraphs, God took me even deeper into my healing. I felt joy bubbling up and mingling with my grief. Overcoming was on the horizon. Light was breaking through.

El Roi

The frequency of Heaven
is the glory of God.

Shining bright, holding tight;
listen close, it's grandiose.

Overwhelming moments
of Love, Peace, and Joy.

Enraptured by my God, El Roi.

The God who sees me,
and holds me tight.

Our hearts beat as One
with the Heavenly lights.

So it is, was, and always will be.
The story of God shining through me.

Candles

The beauty of a candle
isn't so one can stare
and get lost.

The beauty of a candle
is the illumination of the dark,
as it casts forth its light.

The beauty of a candle
allows anyone in its path
the opportunity to see
what was once hidden.

Those sleepwalking turn away
for the brightness hurts their eyes,
but those ready to awaken stand tall,
allowing the candle's flame to light their wick.

Candles of awareness carry on,
dissipating the slumbering darkness,
illuminating all there is, was, and ever will be.

Oh, glorious day when the candles
are glowing so brightly together
no darkness can be found.

I now sit, editing this, in the full warmth of the sun, blades of grass between my toes. White butterflies visit frequently, and with a smile, I call every one "Becky Lynn."

It's been fifteen months, and each day continues to present itself with a more expansive perspective than the day before. All part of the journey—never culminating, forever unfolding.

This is the beauty of a compassionate and gentle God able to turn the gushing grief of loss into floodwaters of love, peace, and joy.

By laying it all out there, the remaining chains that held me down have broken into tiny pieces. I am truly free—able to spread my wings and fly high, up into the sky.

The Valve

Love comes
from only one place,
from only one Source.

Open the valve fully,
and feel the flow of God.

Those we've loved and lost will always be a part of us.
Their presence, etched deep and permanent.
Their love, forever felt.

This truth keeps the drips more gentle when they fall.

Tears

Tears are a cleansing,
a refreshing of the soul;
allow them to rain down.

I found healing to come when I desired it.

As a child of God, it's my birthright.
But I had to claim it down from the heavens—
as my living inheritance.

Heaven's Music

Cast your cares aside,
deep into the depths of the ocean.
Let them sink out of sight where they belong.

Sit with Me awhile; find your rest
in the beauty of creation's song.

The whistling of the wind,
the chirping birds from above.

Sing Heaven's music along with us.
It's Joy. It's Peace. It's Love.

With eyes on Jesus, I clearly see.

God is making all things new, even me.

Patience

Leave the questions open;
let the tension sit.

When God wants to reveal,
He will.

Epilogue
to experience God

On the sixth day after Beck moved to Heaven,
I wrote in my journal...

> *"We come here to experience God
> and help others experience God."*

May my story of loss, grief, and healing help you
navigate your own—your story, too, is one worth exploring.

Higher

Sometimes, through our loss,
we find a new way to live
that lifts us higher.

Faith Walk

One step at a time
is how a faith walk begins
and how courage grows.

Hope

My hope is in God,
the Creator of all things;
nothing else compares.

God Says

I will woo you with My perfect love.
I will hold you tight in My perfect peace.
I will lift you up by My perfect joy.

For you My child, are worthy.

The death of a loved one changes you.
It changes how you view the world.
It causes a seismic shift.

The world you once knew is different
and forever will be.

Whether you saw it coming or it caught you off guard,
there's nothing you can do to change the fact—
the death of a loved one changes you.

How it changes you,
is truly up to you.

poetry index

Intro	Yet I	56	Come Into My Arms
5	Healing Space	59	*Dry
7	White Butterflies	61	Always Found
9	Hymns	65	Hold On
11	Slow Drip	67	To Believe
25	Foggy Mourn	69	Rapids
29	Flooding	71	Mountaintop View
31	Glimmer of Hope	73	Together
35	Language of Tears	79	Whirlwind
40	Words from Heaven	81	Beauty of Tears
43	Storms of Life	83	Sit Awhile
45	Different	85	God's Whisper
47	Black Wings	87	The Cove
51	Without	92	*For All Who Are Lost
53	Sunsetting Nights	95	Wrestling with God

97	*Only God	136	Transitioning Seasons
99	Love Like Water	139	Blessed Are They
101	The Peace that Transcends	143	Love Brings You Home
103	When Lost	145	Be a Diamond
105	Each Day	149	Embrace
107	The Book	155	El Roi
111	With God	157	Candles
115	Be-coming	159	The Valve
119	Throne of Healing	161	Tears
121	Souvenir	163	Heaven's Music
123	Legacy	165	Patience
125	Beauty in the Barren	171	Higher
128	Loss in the Holidays	173	Faith Walk
131	Breaking Through	175	*Hope
133	This Holiday Scene	177	God Says

*originally published in *God Is So Much More: A Poetry Collection*

Also Available

God Is So Much More: A Poetry Collection

The Owl in the Concrete Tree: A Poetry Collection

Stay Connected

angelkwill.com

Angel K Will

enjoys exploring God's glorious creation,
sharing her discoveries through creative works, and
showering those in her midst with love, peace, and joy.

In Loving Memory & Arisen Honor

there are those who leave
impressions on our hearts,
and we're never the same

Angel & Aunt Becky

Tommy & Angel

www.ingramcontent.com/pod-product-compliance
Lightning Source LLC
Chambersburg PA
CBHW060132100426
42744CB00007B/757